IMAGES
*of America*

# LUDLOW

IMAGES
*of America*

# LUDLOW

Judy L. Neff

ARCADIA
PUBLISHING

Published by Arcadia Publishing
Charleston, South Carolina

Library of Congress Catalog Card Number: 2006927404

For all general information contact Arcadia Publishing at:
Telephone 843-853-2070
Fax 843-853-0044
E-mail sales@arcadiapublishing.com
For customer service and orders:
Toll-Free 1-888-313-2665

Visit us on the Internet at www.arcadiapublishing.com

*This book is dedicated to the memory of my late parents, Alma and Jack Neff, who gave to me the enduring gift of a memorable childhood in Ludlow. This work is also a tribute to a man I never knew—Judge John M. Hunnicutt—who in 1935 wrote the book* History of the City of Ludlow, *which seven decades later fascinates me.*

# CONTENTS

# ACKNOWLEDGMENTS

The scarcity of historical photographs contributes greatly to the challenge of compiling a book of this design. I sincerely appreciate the generosity of all individuals and organizations that have allowed me the privilege of using their images in this book. Please know that the absence of a specific item in this work is in no way a reflection of my lack of interest in it or a lack of its significance, but rather it reflects either the nonexistence of a reproducible photograph or sometimes the lack of permission to use it. Thanks to Ed Knue for his many hours of technical support in the reproduction of these photographs, as well as for handling issues when my fickle computer exhibited behavioral problems. Particular credit goes to the Kenton County Public Library, a facility that has put forth great effort in preserving and sharing local history. With his endless supply of knowledge and enthusiasm on the subject, Dave Schroeder, Kentucky history librarian at the Kenton County Public Library, also deserves special recognition. His love of local history is contagious!

# INTRODUCTION

Drawn to its remoteness and beauty, early prosperous families introduced civilization to the land that would later become Ludlow, Kentucky, by establishing their estates here. In some cases, they built summer homes to escape the harsh heat of the South. Many of the streets in Ludlow today still bear the names of some of these early families, including Carneal Street, Kenner Street, Closson Court, and Latta Avenue.

Like many cities in this region, the area was originally part of a governmental land grant. Awarded to Thomas Sandford in 1790, this riverfront land was later traded to Thomas Carneal in exchange for his property located in the vicinity of current Fort Mitchell.

After trading his property with Sandford, Thomas Carneal, a member of the Kentucky Legislature, built Ludlow's oldest surviving home, Elmwood Hall, in 1818. This socially prominent family later sold their exquisite riverfront estate to Englishman William Bullock, a man who had become enthralled with the estate while visiting the area. Bullock had zealous dreams of developing the area into an idyllic town, for which he had chosen the name Hygeia. Planned with much grandeur, the project was platted out by British architect J. B. Papworth. Bullock, however, was unable to convince fellow Englishmen to invest in the project, and his Hygeia remained but a dream. He disappointedly later sold the land to Israel Ludlow. (Ludlow's father, possessing the same name, was a surveyor contracted by the federal government to survey parts of Ohio and is known as one of the founders of Cincinnati.) The Ludlow family, soon to be the namesake for the upcoming city, eventually divided much of their possession into lots that would further populate and characterize the city.

By 1864, a small community had developed, and a request for incorporation was forwarded to the Commonwealth of Kentucky. Historical reports indicate that this request for incorporation was in large part fueled by the frustration of residents surrounding transportation issues. Traveling to adjacent areas was a challenge. Tollbooths hindered travel through both the western and the eastern ends of the area. The ferry service to Cincinnati, run by the William McCoy family, was both unreliable and overpriced. Perturbed residents hoped that incorporating as a city would allow for regulation of ferry service and prices and hopefully alleviate this burden.

The request for incorporation was indeed approved by Frankfort; the charter was received in February 1864, signed by Secretary of State E. L. Van Winkle. At this time, the city named Ludlow, although founded at a much earlier time, was officially born.

As in most cities, Ludlow's earliest history revolves around the development of places of worship and education, and one full chapter of this book is dedicated to these entities. Unique in Ludlow's history, however, are several features. The decision of the Cincinnati Southern Railway to locate in Ludlow changed the face of the city forever. Drawn to the railroad jobs, middle-class families began to arrive, and the population of Ludlow rose dramatically. Over the years, the railroad has gone by several names: the Cincinnati Southern Railway, the Queen and Crescent Railway, and the Cincinnati, New Orleans, and Texas Pacific Railroad (CNO&TPRR) For the sake of simplicity, I refer to the railroad as the Cincinnati Southern Railway throughout the book.

The history of public service in Ludlow likewise is unique. Robert Callahan, the first police chief after elimination of the city marshal position, was reelected repeatedly and held that title for over 40 years. One of Ludlow's early mayors (R. H. Flemming), a Civil War veteran, was elected as an early Kentucky state senator in 1901. A volunteer fire department, organized in 1884, still exists today.

In 1915, a Hollywood-like facility nearly located in picturesque Ludlow. Newspaper articles early that year document competition between Fort Thomas and Ludlow for the location of a new movie film studio. The Highland Film Company would reportedly employ 500 individuals, and negotiations with H. H. McGraw of New York City ensued. At one point, news articles announced that the Lagoon site had been chosen over the Campbell County location. An article in the *Kentucky Post* on March 23, 1915, stated, "We will first erect the $1,000,000 studio on the high elevation back of the Lagoon, across the tracks of the Southern Railroad, and administration buildings on the Lagoon property, forming a massive entrance to the park." More specific plans for the transformation included replacing the center of the Motordrome with a revolving stage, and it was proclaimed that "a portion of the lake will be made into a miniature Venice, with bridges and gondolas." Newspapers enthusiastically claimed that this was to be the moving picture center of the Mississippi Valley. Later, however, it was reported that the nearly-100-acre site in Fort Thomas, on Grand Avenue between Highland and Fort Thomas Avenues, had instead been chosen over the Ludlow site for the moving picture "city." In the end, shortly after one news article proclaimed the "deal nearly closed," came the announcement in July 1916 that the Highland Film Company was disbanding, bring an end to the fervent newspaper articles.

Undoubtedly, when reminiscing on the history of Ludlow, the spotlight always falls to the Lagoon Amusement Park. The park thrived from 1895 to 1918, entertaining thousands at a time with rides, game booths, a dance pavilion, boating, vaudeville, a moving picture theater, and more. Three unfortunate consecutive happenings eventually contributed to the amusement park's demise. A deadly accident and fire at the motorcycle track, a merciless tornado in 1915, and the onset of Prohibition ultimately brought the excitement to a conclusion.

Now, nearly a century and a half since incorporation, Ludlow still gracefully sits along the southern banks of the muddy Ohio River, full of citizens proud of the small town's past but equally enthusiastic about its future.

# One

# CITY SCENES

A view of Elm Street, near its intersection with Locust Street and heading toward West Covington, shows the Ritchie family home on the left and the Ludlow Christian Church on the right. A rare glimpse of the Ludlow Railroad Depot can be seen as you follow the road to the top of the picture. The photograph was taken on November 6, 1896, the week of Pres. William McKinley and Vice Pres. Garret Hobart's election. (Courtesy of the Kenton County Public Library.)

Spanning over Pleasant Run Creek, this wooden bridge connecting Ludlow and Bromley was once a toll bridge. (Courtesy of the Kenton County Public Library.)

The *Kenton* provided ferry service to Ludlow residents, docking near the Southern Railway Bridge. At one time, this ferry also served as Covington's Main Street Ferry. (Courtesy of the Kenton County Public Library.)

One of Ludlow's most significant fires occurred on July 26, 1892, when a resin refinery owned by the H. C. Garlick Company burned. According to newspaper reports, it smoldered for quite some time and wasn't entirely put out until September 5. The business was located near the south end of the Cincinnati Southern Railway Bridge. This is a view of Elm Street looking eastward toward the inferno. (Courtesy of the Kenton County Public Library.)

In 1893, this Fourth of July parade passed under the Cincinnati Southern Railway Bridge heading to Ash Street. Early in Ludlow's history, Ash Street was an important thoroughfare and an active business area. (Courtesy of the Kenton County Public Library.)

The Ludlow property, in Kentucky, opposite Mill Creek, was sold in part Tuesday, by Wright and Graff; about one hundred acres were disposed of in lots by the acre, and foot front. 15 lots were sold at from $3.00 to $6.75 per foot, and eleven at the rate of from $130 to $275 per acre Total amount of sales $25,000. *Cin. Times,*

On June 18, 1847, the *Licking Valley Register* reported the sale of parcels of the Ludlow property. At one point, Israel Ludlow owned nearly 1,200 acres in the area now known as the City of Ludlow. By the time of this sale, he had already sold a 42-acre plot to his brother-in-law George Kenner. (Courtesy of the Kenton County Public Library.)

Heavy rains in 1894 delayed the process of grading Elm Street for the streetcar tracks. (Courtesy of the Kenton County Public Library.)

Even the children celebrated on the day the Ludlow car line was opened—September 22, 1894. Included in the picture are some of the children of the Ritchie family. (Courtesy of the Kenton County Public Library.)

Ludlow residents look on as one of the first streetcars to service the city passes by on September 22, 1894, at what is now the 100 block of Elm Street. (Courtesy of the Kenton County Public Library.)

A view of Elm Street *c.* 1898 shows pedestrian traffic under the K. F. Bresnan store sign. Kate F. Bresnan is listed in the city directories as a saleslady and shoe dealer. Two crossing streetcars are seen on the right. (Courtesy of the Earl Clark Collection.)

Some recognizable large homes on Highway Avenue were photographed when they were new. The Montclair Street area is under construction on the left. (Courtesy of the Kenton County Public Library.)

Further down Highway Avenue, a scarcity of houses is evident. Both sides of this street are now lined with homes. (Courtesy of the Kenton County Public Library.)

This spectacular view of Ludlow includes the steeple of St. Boniface Church and the Ludlow Public School building on the left. The photograph was taken from the south side of the railroad tracks, from a site near Ludlow's new River's Breeze Condominium development. (Courtesy of the Kenton County Public Library.)

A streetcar traverses a trestle during the construction of the Elm Street viaduct in 1917. (Courtesy of the Kenton County Public Library.)

Motorman Andy Goetz and conductor P. J. Collopy are seen inside a streetcar at the entrance to the Lagoon Amusement Park. A special loop of track was installed for the purpose of servicing the park, with up to 50 vehicles needed daily during peak months. The loop of tracks deviated off of Oak Street, going south on Lake Street, east on Laurel Street, and then north again onto Deverill Street to return to the main tracks on Oak Street. This car is representative of one of the company's "convertible style" vehicles, with the windows removed for the summer months. (Courtesy of the Earl Clark Collection.)

During World War II, civilian war efforts included scrap drives, introducing Americans to the early process of recycling. These victory boxes for the collection of scrap were placed throughout Ludlow. (Courtesy of the Hellebush family.)

Looking west into Bromley, a streetcar is seen standing at the end of the line at the Bromley loop at Shelby and Pleasant Streets in 1939. Streetcars circled the small square structure on the right, the Mary Lee Beauty Salon. (Courtesy of the Earl Clark Collection.)

Route 3 is prominently displayed on this streetcar at the Bromley loop in 1939, a designation still used for the Ludlow TANK (Transit Authority of Northern Kentucky) buses today. (Courtesy of the Earl Clark Collection.)

Onlookers at 213 Elm Street await the parade during Ludlow's 75th anniversary celebration in 1939. (Courtesy of the Hellebush family.)

Participating in the 75th anniversary parade in 1939, Ludlow residents appear to be enjoying the streetcar ride. Pictured are, from left to right, Dorothy Kilgore (later Cartwright), Madeline Grieme (later Corbett), Marcella Schrage, Michael Rohan, and Jane Rohan (later Bodkin). (Courtesy of the Earl Clark Collection.)

Submerged during the 1937 flood is the intersection of Elm and Adela Streets. The river crested at 79.9 feet that year. (Courtesy of the Schachere family.)

Damage was revealed as the floodwaters receded at the corner of Kenner and Hooper Streets. A house sits on its side in Kenner Street. Trumbull Electric Manufacturing Company is seen on the right, a building now occupied by Spati Industries. (Courtesy of Spati Industries.)

Entering 818 Oak Street by canoe is Betty Clements (later Bodkin) on the right and Lucille Tremain on the left. The man in the center is unidentified. (Courtesy of the Louis Bodkin family.)

Floodwaters in 1937 filled some homes on Oak Street nearly to the roof. This view is at the intersection of Oak and Park Streets looking north. (Courtesy of the Louis Bodkin family.)

A group looks across the frozen Ohio River at Ludlow in the early 1900s. The large Ludlow Public School building can be seen on the far right. (Courtesy of the Kenton County Public Library.)

Many still remember the days when Ludlow Park had a public wading pool. The pool was an addition to the park in 1931. Constructed on land donated by the Ludlow family, the park is named Albert S. Ludlow Memorial Park in honor of the son of Israel Ludlow. (Courtesy of John and Janet Gaiser; photograph by Raymond Hadorn; used with permission of the Hadorn family.)

# *Two*

# PUBLIC SERVICE

James Peak was Ludlow's city marshal from 1888 to 1892. The city marshal post was eventually abolished and replaced with the chief of police position in 1894. (Courtesy of the Kenton County Public Library.)

A multitalented individual, T. J. McNeal was Ludlow's mayor from 1888 to 1892 as well as a carpenter and attorney, according to early city directories. He lived on Carneal Street. (Courtesy of the Kenton County Public Library.)

Identified on Elm Street are Mr. Howard (left) and R. H. Flemming (right). Flemming served as Ludlow's mayor from 1883 to 1888 and again from 1893 to 1901. In 1901, he was elected Kentucky state senator. Prior to settling in Ludlow, he participated in the Civil War as a member of the 77th Ohio Regiment. Injured during the Battle of Shiloh, Flemming entered service as a private and left with the rank of captain. His funeral in 1907 was described by the *Kentucky Post* as the "largest funeral ever in Ludlow." (Courtesy of the Kenton County Public Library.)

Andrew J. Hughes was one of Ludlow's early mail carriers. (Courtesy of the Kenton County Public Library.)

Having previously been located in a smaller building on Elm Street, Ludlow's post office moved into this building at the northwest corner of Kenner and Elm Streets in 1922. The current postal facility at 640 Elm Street was built in 1963. At one time, the pictured building was also known as the Woolford Building, and Schrage's Hardware Store was once located here. A convenience store currently occupies the site. (Courtesy of Barb Lindle.)

Robert Callahan held the position of police chief for an unprecedented number of years. Serving as city marshal since 1892, he was elected to the newly formed office of chief of police in 1894, a position he retained until 1936. Callahan was elected during Ludlow's first secret vote, known as the kangaroo system or the Australian ballot system. He was born in Harrison, Ohio, and is buried at St. Mary's Cemetery in Fort Mitchell. (Courtesy of Lt. Col. Benny Johnson.)

At the age of 73, Chief Robert Callahan died on August 16, 1936, at his home at 421 Oak Street, with bronchopneumonia and carcinoma of the tongue. He had ceased active duty only one month prior. Several days later, Harvey Searp was appointed by city council to take over as Ludlow's second chief of police. This headline appeared in the *Kentucky Post* on August 17, 1936. (Courtesy of the Kenton County Public Library.)

# LUDLOW CHIEF DIES AT HOME AFTER ILLNESS

### Career of 44 Years as Head of Police Department Is Ended by Death

### LAST RITES ARE ARRANGED

### Members of Fire Department to Pay Last Respects at Residence Tuesday

Members of the Ludlow Fire Department c. 1892 are seen with Police Chief Robert Callahan (second from left). Two other individuals listed on the photograph are Mike Jordan and Mike Nolan, although their order is not clear. (Courtesy of the Kenton County Public Library.)

SAM'L E. WEST

Candidate for

**Chief of Police**

For City of Ludlow, Ky.

Earnestly Solicits Your Vote.

Election, Tuesday, November 2nd, 1909.

**Saml. E. West**

ift ein Kandidat für **Polizei-Chef,** von Ludlow,
Ky. Wahl am Dienstag, den 2. November 1909.

Samuel E. West challenged Chief Callahan in the 1909 election for chief of police; his endeavor was unsuccessful. Note the bottom half of his card is printed in German. (Courtesy of Chief Ray Murphy.)

Labeled "old pump crew of Ludlow Fire Co.," this photograph is dated 1885. In earlier years, two rival fire companies had existed in Ludlow—the Citizens Fire Brigade and the George Washington Fire Company. (Courtesy of the Kenton County Public Library.)

Ludlow's city hall and firehouse on Oak Street were photographed around 1890. These structures existed until 1923, when they were replaced with a brick building that housed both entities. Fire equipment and the police department were located on the first floor; a large city council hall occupied the second floor. The 1923 structure remains the site of the current firehouse. (Courtesy of the Kenton County Public Library.)

With their horse-drawn fire equipment, the Ludlow Fire Department is seen in front of the city hall building and firehouse on Oak Street in 1918. A year earlier, the department had purchased their first motorized piece of equipment. (Courtesy of the Kenton County Public Library.)

David Grimmeissen was a member of the fire department from age 18 until his death at the age of 57. He is seen here with Prince and Major, the last two horses to serve with the fire department. By 1926, they were retired; motorized equipment had taken over their jobs. (Courtesy of the Kenton County Public Library.)

# *Three*

# BUSINESSES

Amos Teed stands in front of his shoe store. Born in England, he learned shoemaking from his father and came to the United States at age 14. Besides shoemaking, he also served on the Ludlow School Board and was president of the Farmers and Mechanics Bank (later the Bank of Ludlow). Teed retired from the shoe business in 1923 and later was elected to the office of mayor, defeating opponent George Vandeventer. He took office on January 1, 1926, and died later that same year. (Courtesy of the Kenton County Public Library.)

John Ramler operated a grocery store on Linden Street. This building is at 436 Linden Street (previously known as 114 Linden Street, prior to address numbering changes that took place throughout Ludlow in 1921). The structure currently houses apartments. (Courtesy of the Schachere family.)

Romanowitz Grocery Store was located on Elm Street next to the old Odd Fellows' Hall. If it still stood today, it would be adjacent to the Huntington Bank property. (Courtesy of the Kenton County Public Library.)

Max Cleveland, a grocer, made deliveries throughout Ludlow in his horse-drawn wagon. His store was located on Elm Street. (Courtesy of the Kenton County Public Library.)

The *Ludlow Reporter* on August 15, 1874, contained an advertisement listing services available at Hugo Stahl's apothecary. His business was located on the southwest corner of Elm and Carneal Streets, supplying products from varnishes to medicines. (Courtesy of the Special Collections and Archives, Northern Kentucky University.)

ELM AND CARNEAL,]                    [LUDLOW, KY.

## HUGO STAHL,

DRUGGIST AND APOTHECARY, would respectfully announce to the people of Ludlow, Ky., and vicinity that he will keep always on hand a complete assortment of

| DRUGS, | CHEMICALS, |
| PATENT MEDICINES, | PERFUMES, |
| TOILET AND | FANCY ARTICLES, |
| SOAPS AND | BRUSHES, |
| OILS, PAINTS, | AND VARNISHES, |

&c., &c., &c.

Pure Wines and Liquors for Medicinal Purposes Exclusively.

☞ Physicians' Prescriptions carefully compounded day and night.

Fred Werges established his boot and shoe business in the late 1800s. The building still stands at 216 Elm Street (previously known as 62 Elm Street). Mr. and Mrs. Werges are pictured with their son Fred Jr., on the right. (Courtesy of the Kenton County Public Library.)

A view of the Odd Fellows' Hall at the northeast corner of Elm and Butler Streets is seen. The building was constructed in 1889 and demolished in 1971. Businesses operating in the building just prior to its razing were the Rock Bar Café and Pop's Pool Hall. Huntington Bank now occupies the site. In the distance at left is a glimpse of the Ludlow Bazaar, identified by the writing on the side of the building. (Courtesy of Barb Lindle.)

The Farmers and Mechanics Bank is depicted on this etching from a large paperclip. Note the bank's capital of a whopping $30,000. The bank operated out of the first floor of the Odd Fellows' Hall on Elm Street. Listed are bank president Amos Teed and cashier T. W. Balsly. Balsly, a cashier for over 20 years, was also Ludlow mayor from 1918 to 1922. He later admitted to the embezzlement of nearly $80,000 in 1926, which led to temporary bank closure. In the face of criminal charges, he committed suicide in the basement of the bank on September 30, 1926, at the age of 53. The bank later became the Bank of Ludlow, surviving only until 1931. (Author's collection.)

The demolition of the Odd Fellows' Hall at Elm and Butler Streets regrettably took place in 1971. The historic Bentley House (now Ronald B. Jones Funeral Home) is seen to the left. (Courtesy of the Kenton County Public Library.)

ELMWOOD HALL   HOME OF . . .

*Mrs. Thomas' Candies*

"Always Good Taste"

Since 1920

BUILT IN 1818
FIRST HOME IN LUDLOW, KY.   244 Forest Ave.   Phone: 261-9197

Mrs. Thomas' Candies operated out of 244 Forest Avenue, known as Elmwood Hall, from 1920 until 1971. Candy made here was sold widely throughout the area, including in the Dixie Terminal and at Shillito's Department Store in downtown Cincinnati. The home was built by Thomas Carneal c. 1818 on land that later became the city of Ludlow. (Courtesy of Paula Reynolds.)

Mrs. Thomas' Candies was a family-run business founded by Edna E. Vogelsang Thomas. After retiring and closing the business, she moved to Fort Mitchell. (Courtesy of the Kenton County Public Library.)

Nick and George Braun operated a saloon on the southeast corner of Ash and Carneal Streets during the late 1800s. By 1904, the property is listed in the city directory as housing the Carpenter and Rigdon saloon. The building still exists, although the one seen to the left is gone. (Courtesy of the Kenton County Public Library.)

This handwritten entry of Mayor R. H. Flemming from the Mayor Court of Ludlow grants Nick Braun a license to sell "spirituous, vinous and malt liquors" on September 23, 1885. (Courtesy of the Kenton County Public Library.)

# Ludlow  Reporter

VOLUME 2.        LUDLOW, KY., JULY 17, 1875.        NUMBER 12.

The *Ludlow Reporter* was published only during 1874 and 1875 by Marine R. Gravener, a Ludlow grocer. Gravener utilized space in the newspaper to advertise goods sold at his store at the southwest corner of Elm and Carneal Streets. (Courtesy of the Special Collections and Archives, Northern Kentucky University.)

In this undated photograph, a parade vehicle sponsored by Schrage Hardware promotes support for the playground. (Courtesy of David Schrage.)

Bernard and Magdalen Schrage established their Ludlow business in 1920 when they purchased a hardware store from the Gerwe family. This was their original location at 241 Elm Street. Pictured from left to right are Bernard Schrage, Magdalen Schrage, Joe Gerwe, and Henrietta Gerwe. Sitting in the wagon in the front is Dick Schrage. (Courtesy of David Schrage.)

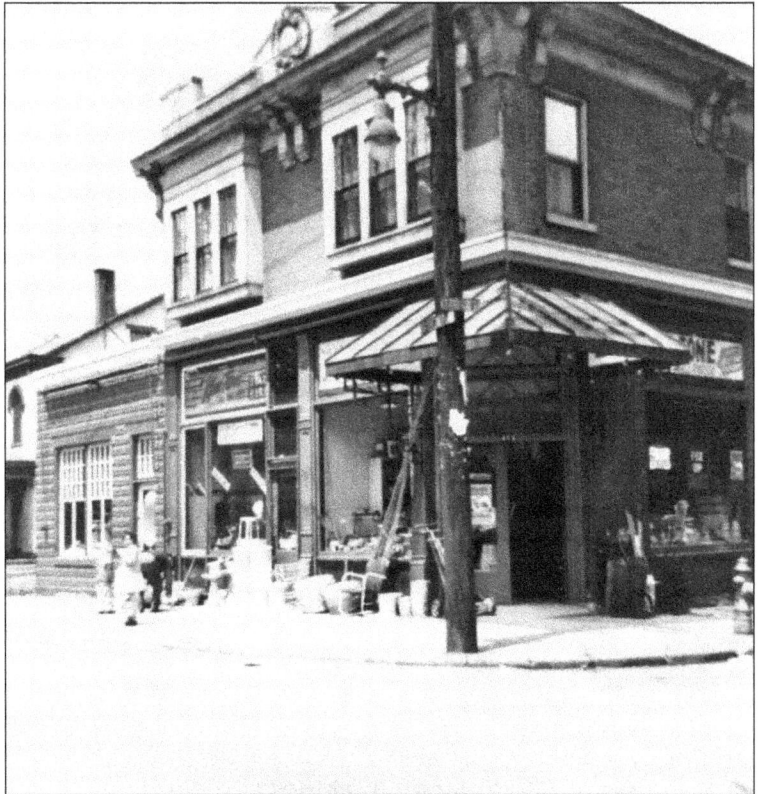

A later location of Schrage Hardware Store at Elm and Kenner Streets is shown. Another photograph on page 25 shows this same building when it was occupied by the post office. (Courtesy of David Schrage.)

John McCormick, pictured *c.* 1892, was one of Ludlow's early druggists. His business was later taken over by the Farrell family. (Courtesy of the Kenton County Public Library.)

John McCormick is seen in the doorway of his pharmacy at the northeast corner of Elm Street and Euclid Avenue. Early in Ludlow's history, Euclid Avenue was called George Street, with the name change taking place in 1910. (Courtesy of the Farrell family.)

Laying of the cornerstone for the Masonic Temple at the northeast corner of Elm Street and Euclid Avenue took place on May 14, 1884. It would be the first three-story building in Ludlow. (Courtesy of the Kenton County Public Library.)

A very early, undated view of the Masonic Temple at Elm Street and Euclid Avenue shows the building with its steeple-like structure still intact. According to an article in the *Daily Commonwealth*, the lower floors were "devoted to mercantile pursuits," with Samuel Reed Lodge F&AM utilizing the third floor. Identifiable on the right side of the building is Gibbs and Robinson, declared as "dealers in staple and fancy groceries" per the city directory. This building is currently home to Tom Gaither's Studio/Gallery. (Courtesy of the Farrell family.)

Farrell's Pharmacy had taken over the McCormick business by the time of this photograph. The men pictured in front of the location at Elm Street and Euclid Avenue are unidentified. (Courtesy of the Farrell family.)

Edward Farrell Sr. established Farrell's Pharmacy in Ludlow in 1908. Children Edward Jr., Mary, and Agnes all became pharmacists as well, with Mary and Agnes being among some of the earliest women pharmacists in Kentucky. Farrell's Pharmacy later merged with Ludlow Family Pharmacy, where William Farrell Jr. carries on the family tradition. (Courtesy of the Farrell family.)

A postcard shows Farrell's Pharmacy as well as numerous other businesses located on Elm Street east of Euclid Avenue. (Courtesy of the Farrell family.)

Blanche Schachere stands among a variety of merchandise sold at the Schachere's confectionary in 1941. The store was located at 602 West Oak Street, later to be owned by John H. Schulte. Currently JD's Deli operates here. (Courtesy of the Schachere family.)

Jack Hellebush (left) and Joe Jeffries (right) stand among cans of paint inside the Hellebush family's original paint store, which was located on the south side of Elm Street. The business was purchased from the Donathorn Paint Company in 1928. (Courtesy of the Hellebush family.)

Charles Moore Jr. (left), William Earl Hellebush (center), and Robert Moore (right) stand in front of Hellebush's Ludlow Paint Store at 212 Elm Street c. 1940. This was the second location on Elm Street for the business. (Courtesy of the Hellebush family.)

Exonumia is the study of coin-like objects, such as tokens and medals. Trade tokens have recently become popular collectible items. As seen in this image, many Ludlow businesses were promoted with these types of tokens. (Courtesy of Carl Rekow and Ed Kleier.)

Edward Monahan operated Monahan's Carry-Out with his wife, Marie, at 601 Church Street. Many residents remember the store's endless supply of penny candy. Prior to his death in 2001, Monahan was very active in both civic and church affairs. He held numerous positions, including grand knight of the Kehoe Council Knights of Columbus, city council member, and mayor. Mr. Monahan is pictured inside the store in May 1953. (Courtesy of the Monahan family.)

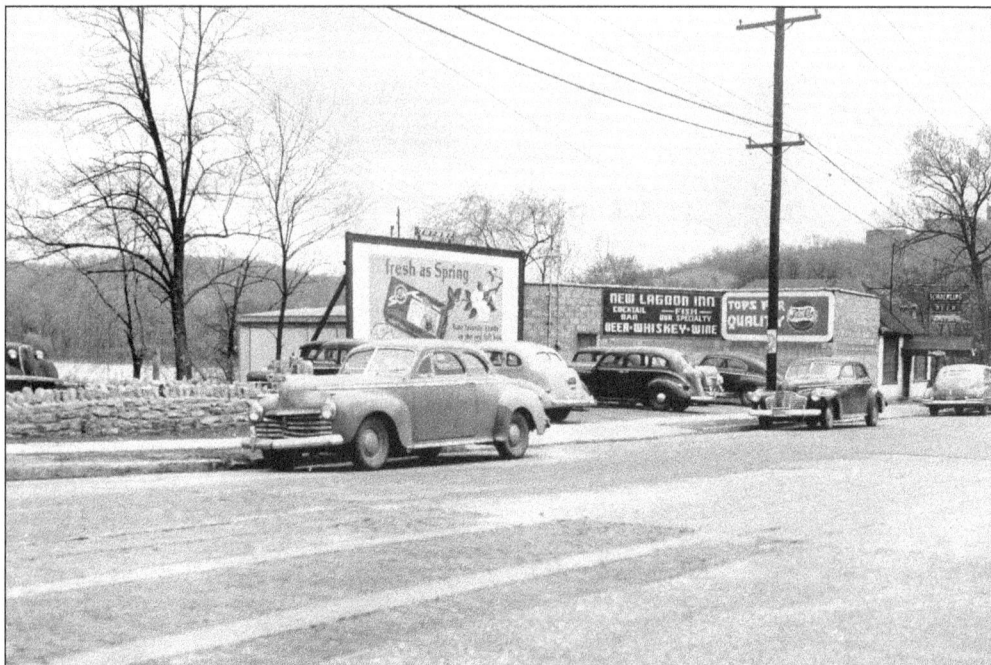

Business appears to be booming at the New Lagoon Inn at Oak and Lagoon Streets. The most recent business occupying this site was a bingo hall. (Courtesy of the Hellebush family.)

A baseball team sponsored by A. H. Ross and Company was photographed in front of their building located at the intersection of Kenner and Hooper Streets. They were a manufacturer of packaging equipment. The building was later occupied by various businesses, including Trumbull Electric and Cincinnati Trailer Sales, Inc. The structure is now home to Spati Industries, Inc., designers and manufacturers of special machinery. (Courtesy of David Schrage.)

# _Four_

# CITIZENS

Mrs. Closson, Mrs. Price, Mrs. Massar, and Mrs. Latta are included in this group photograph outside of the Closson home. Their order is unclear, and the fifth woman is unidentified. (Courtesy of the Kenton County Public Library.)

Elmwood Hall is known as Ludlow's first permanent residence and is the oldest surviving building in Ludlow. An early view of Elmwood Hall shows the back of the home (now utilized as the front) before alterations were made, dating this image to the 1870s. Built c. 1818 by Thomas Carneal, the home was a part of a large estate that spanned nearly two and a half miles along the Kentucky side of the Ohio River, on land that would later become Ludlow. The wing seen on the left was removed in the 1880s. Close inspection of the photograph reveals two women on the porch, identified as Miss Mewhinney and Ida Nixon. Seen in the yard are the Nixon children. (Courtesy of Patrick Snadon.)

Seen in this photograph are Mrs. Proctor D. Patrick (left) and Mrs. William Wahle (right). This photograph was likely taken around 1890, as the home had undergone some alterations by this time. Specifically the house had been partitioned into a duplex. Seen here again is the original back of the home, now considered the front, which faces Forest Avenue. (Courtesy of Patrick Snadon.)

Elmwood Hall was home to Mrs. Thomas' Candies from 1920 until 1971. An unidentified person peers through the door on the right in this wintertime view. The home still exists as a private residence at 244 Forest Avenue. (Courtesy of the Kenton County Public Library.)

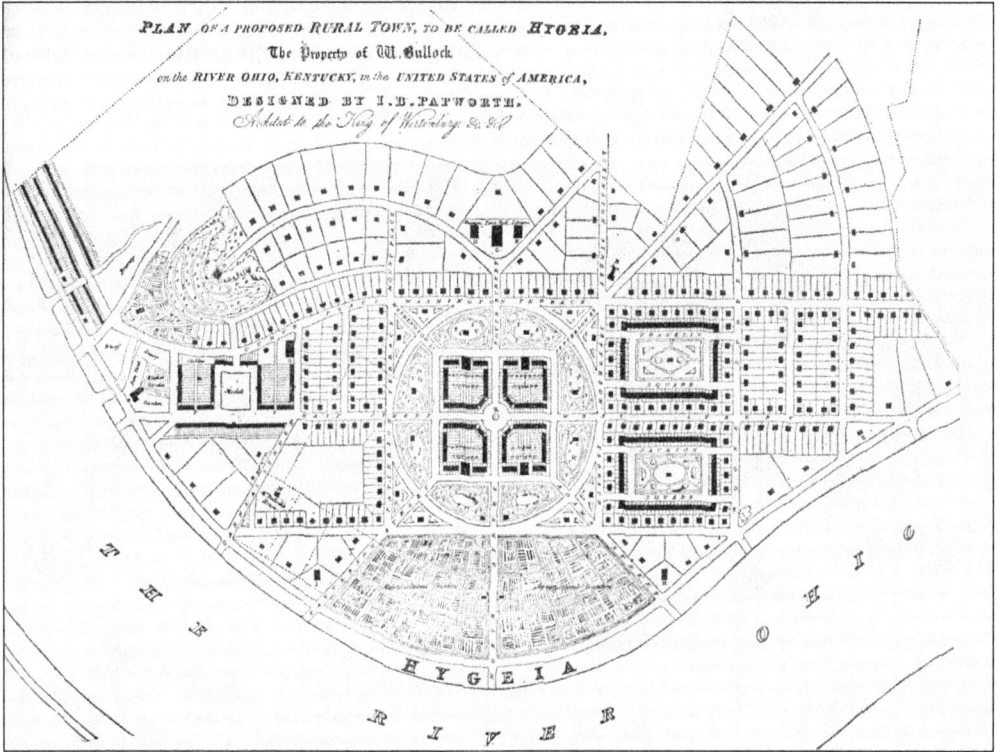

Around 1827, Thomas Carneal sold Elmwood Hall to its second owner, Englishman William Bullock, who had become enthralled with the estate during a visit to the area. Bullock hired J. B. Papworth to design a town he intended to establish on the land, to be named Hygeia (in Greek mythology, Hygeia was the goddess of health). When Bullock was unsuccessful selling lots to other British investors, his grand plan never materialized. In 1831, he sold Elmwood Hall to Israel Ludlow Jr., who eventually became the city's namesake. (Courtesy of Patrick Snadon.)

Rev. James Work tutors members of the Closson family on the front steps of their home, known as Somerset Hall. A. B. Closson Jr., their father, was the founder of A. B. Closson Jr. Company on Fourth Street in Cincinnati, selling maps, charts, and artwork. The Closson family lived here from 1885 to 1925. (Courtesy of the Chapman family.)

Another view of the Closson home showcases the extraordinarily long back porch. The home was built in 1832 by the Kenner family; other owners have included Thomas Keevan and Richard Clayton. In 1925, the Closson family sold the property to the Unity Lodge No. 478 F&AM. It was utilized as the Masonic Lodge for many years and is now restored as a private residence. (Courtesy of Barb Lindle.)

Mr. Turner, seen in the 1880s, was one of Ludlow's early lamplighters. Twenty-six posts with kerosene lamps were installed throughout Ludlow in 1872. Lights were lit at dusk and extinguished each midnight. Ludlow's first electric streetlights arrived in 1898. (Courtesy of the Kenton County Public Library.)

Edward Margileth lived at the northwest corner of George Street (later Euclid Avenue) and Forest Avenue. The city directory lists his occupation as traveling salesman. (Courtesy of the Kenton County Public Library.)

Identified in this photograph dated 1911 is Harvey Searp, likely on the grounds of the Lagoon Amusement Park, as he was know to have worked at one of the pony tracks on park grounds. He resided at 382 West Oak Street. His son, also named Harvey Searp, became the second police chief of Ludlow. (Courtesy of the Hellebush family.)

John Birkenkamp operated a saloon at the southwest corner of Ash and Locust Streets during the late 1880s. He was also a member of city council in 1878–1879. (Courtesy of the Kenton County Public Library.)

Two older Ludlow structures, now designated as 107 and 109/111 Elm Street, are pictured in 1889 when Elm Street was still a dirt road and before the installation of streetcar tracks. Both houses still exist with few exterior alterations. (Courtesy of the Kenton County Public Library.)

Mr. Blackburn stopped for a photo opportunity at Elm Street near Euclid Avenue. (Courtesy of the Kenton County Public Library.)

The "Cock Robin" group, as they called themselves, assembled in front of the Ritchie family home at Locust and Elm Streets. (Courtesy of the Kenton County Public Library.)

A photograph of one of Ludlow's amateur football teams *c.* 1900 identified members as follows: Darling, Stubbs, J. Burnett, Dave Buchanan, Joe Cooke, W. Closson, Curly Mershon, W. Davis, Henry Davis, Charles Knosp, Blake Raymond, and Hilary Graves. (Courtesy of the Kenton County Public Library.)

Pictured in his sleigh, Dr. R. H. Crisler was an early Ludlow physician. His combination office and home was on Elm Street, between Carneal and Davies Streets. (Courtesy of the Kenton County Public Library.)

Dr. R. H. Crisler (right) is seen with D. S. Buchanan at a frequently photographed site on Elm Street c. 1913. Mr. Buchanan served on an early city council. Dr. Crisler was also city treasurer from 1897 to 1901. (Courtesy of the Kenton County Public Library.)

The unusual Latta residence was built *c.* 1900 by G. Taylor Latta, son of A. B. Latta. G. Taylor Latta worked as superintendent of the city waterworks. The unique structure possesses 12 equal sides and still stands as a private residence at the northeast corner of Latta Avenue and Butler Street. (Courtesy of the Kenton County Public Library.)

A. B. Latta was an early Ludlow resident who is known for inventing the steam-powered fire engine depicted here. His home was at the same site as the 12-sided structure noted above, but it was demolished when his son built the new home. A. B. Latta was also elected president of Ludlow's first city council in 1864. He died in Ludlow in 1865. (Courtesy of the Kenton County Public Library.)

The Ritchie family home stood at the northwest corner of Locust and Elm Streets, photographed here on January 18, 1888. Casper Ritchie Jr. moved from the family home in Mount Adams to Ludlow, and this structure was completed in 1860 by contractors Shannon and Lukens. His father, Casper Ritchie Sr., eventually joined him in Ludlow in 1866. A convenience store and gas station now occupy the lot (previously an IGA). (Courtesy of the Kenton County Public Library.)

The Ritchie family is seen here inside their Ludlow home on Thanksgiving Day, 1901. Casper Sr. is seated in the back, next to the two women on the right. (Courtesy of the Kenton County Public Library.)

Members of the Ritchie family are identified outside their home at Locust and Elm Streets in 1888. From left to right are (seated) Rob, Casper Sr. holding Casper and Louise, Mrs. Rumsey, Jessie, Harvey, and Luly; (standing) Walter T., Glenna, Effie, Casper Jr., Lily, Mary, and Arnold. Harvey can be seen holding the trip cord to the camera. Walter was an attorney and real-estate agent; Harvey was a machinist and draftsman; Lily and Luly were teachers. (Courtesy of the Kenton County Public Library.)

The Ritchie family grounds were quite extensive and included a stable, carriage house, and cottage for the hired hand. The greenhouse and library are shown here in June 1885. (Courtesy of the Kenton County Public Library.)

The Ritchie family pose themselves outside their Ludlow home at Locust and Elm Streets in this beautifully composed photograph. (Courtesy of the Kenton County Public Library.)

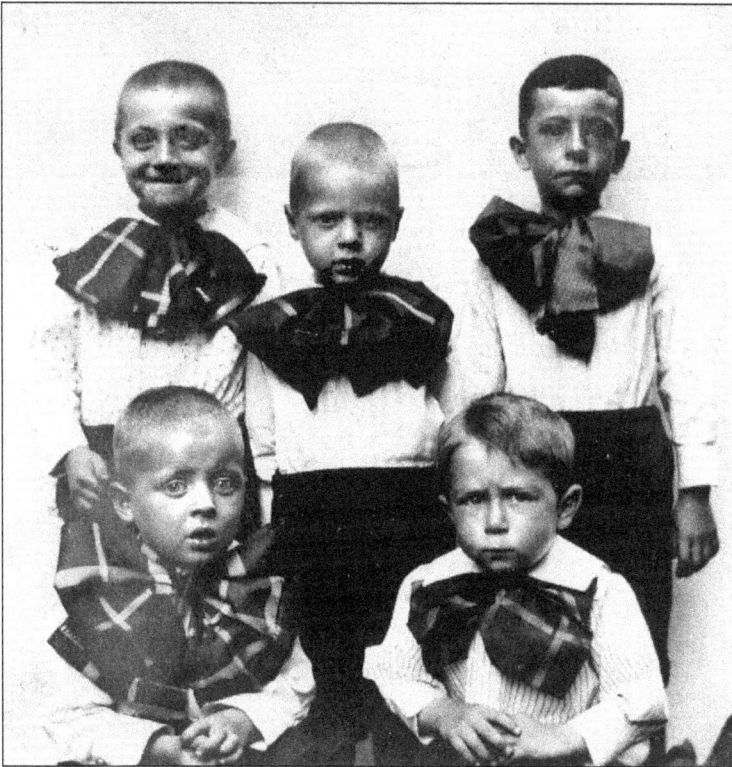

Ritchie children are identified as, from left to right, (first row) Edgar and Walter; (second row) Casper, Andrew, and Morris. Edgar Ritchie grew up to serve in the 355th Infantry during World War I. One year after his enlistment, he was killed in action in Beney, France, on September 15, 1918. As the first Ludlow resident to die in World War I, he was honored by Ludlow's American Legion when it was established in 1919 as the Edgar B. Ritchie Post 25. (Courtesy of the Kenton County Public Library.)

This residence at 859 Oak Street is architecturally described in the National Register of Historic Places as "exotic revival." It was built c. 1920 by Elmer Browning, a cement contractor. (Courtesy of the Hellebush family.)

Another unique Ludlow home at 855/857 Oak Street is located next door to the one shown at left. Also built by Elmer Browning c. 1920, it is described as "mission/Spanish revival" style and is also listed on the National Register of Historic Places. (Courtesy of the Hellebush family.)

A closer 1945 view of 855/857 Oak Street shows the beautiful exterior detail of the home. At the top of the steps is Marcella Staunch. Below, from left to right, are William F. Hellebush, Martha Hellebush, Margaret Hellebush, and Nanny Hellebush. (Courtesy of the Hellebush family.)

The grounds of the Ludlow Springs Hobo Club are pictured, located off of Adela Street near the railroad tracks. This civic organization for men was established c. 1966. Charitable activities included providing Christmas gifts for needy children and sponsoring picnics for various school classes. An actual spring on the property reportedly provided fresh water for many residents during the 1937 flood. (Courtesy of Ed Kleier.)

"The Hobo King," Harry Messer, is seen here in 1981. Messer was one of the founders of the Ludlow Springs Hobo Club. (Courtesy of the Kenton County Public Library.)

In 1917, the Ludlow Giants baseball team included, from left to right, (first row) W. Murphy (pitcher), F. Lincke (center field), J. Hellebush (mascot), F. Grothaus (right field), and W. Hellebush (third base); (second row) D. Buckley (left field), V. Wainscott (first base), H. Clare (catcher), L. Wooley (manager), H. Lowe (second base), J. Crittenden (utility), and A. Morris (shortstop). (Courtesy of the Hellebush family.)

The Ramler sisters of Ludlow—from left to right, Kathleen, Blanche, and Edna—are shown in their Sunday best in this undated photograph. (Courtesy of the Schachere family.)

Anne Lee Patterson of Ludlow won the title of Miss United States of America in 1931 and was subsequently runner-up in the Miss Universe competition. Her family lived at 29 Kenner Street; she attended St. James Elementary School and LaSalette Academy in Covington. She later performed in the Ziegfeld Follies in New York City. After her marriage to Joseph Bandler, the couple moved to California. (Courtesy of the Kenton County Public Library.)

# Five

# THE RAILROAD

Photographed from the south side of the railroad tracks, this postcard gives a panoramic view of a large portion of Ludlow. St. Boniface Church is seen on the left; a partial glimpse of the railroad water towers is on the far right. An interesting aspect in this image is the first row of houses. They stand on Cherry Street, a street that no longer exists in Ludlow. The Cincinnati Southern Railway purchased all of the property and the street in order to expand their facilities, and Cherry Street was no more. (Courtesy of Carl Rekow.)

# The Covington Journal.

## COVINGTON, KY.

### SATURDAY, FEBRUARY 14, 1874.

## LOCATION OF THE SOUTHERN RAILROAD.

### The Ludlow Route Adopted.

The Trustees of the Cincinnati Southern railroad officially announce the location of the road on the Ludlow route. —This location makes Florence a point, and thence along the Lexington Pike, crossing the Short Line at Walton, to Roberts' Store, twenty miles from Covington, to which point, running North, the route had already been located.

The reasons assigned by the Trustees for adopting the Ludlow route are, in brief, its comparative cheapness, a liberal donation of land at Ludlow, and the doubt about getting authority to erect a bridge over the Ohio at Willow Run.

Consolation is offered to Covington in the following statement of the Trustees:

This route [the Willow Run] would probably have suited the majority of the people of Covington better than either of the others, as it was supposed it would afford them more convenient depot grounds; and it is the wish of the Trustees, if possible, to accommodate the wants of that growing city. While they have not yet been able to do so by the selection of the Willow Run crossing, they have had surveyed and procured most of the necessary right of way for a short branch, which they are advised by their consulting engineer will be equally good for its passenger business, and better for its manufacturing interests.

This, the most important act of the Trustees, in connection with the location of the route, was left to the last moment, and then hurriedly done.

It is quite manifest that the Trustees themselves have doubts as to the propriety of their action.

An entry in the *Covington Journal* on February 14, 1874, announces the decision of the Cincinnati Southern Railroad to locate in Ludlow. Railroad officials offered consolation to Covington, the other city competing for the privilege. Acreage donated by the Ludlow family is said to have played a major role in this determination. This decision changed Ludlow from a rural town comprised mostly of affluent families into a middle-class working community. (Courtesy of the Kenton County Public Library.)

James Summers (left) puts in a day's work on the railroad around 1890. He lived at the northwest corner of Adela and Linden Streets. The man on the right is unidentified. (Courtesy of the Kenton County Public Library.)

Five more railroad workers are viewed in this *c.* 1880 image. (Courtesy of the Kenton County Public Library.)

Two very early views of the railroad in Ludlow preserve interesting images of the tollhouse *c.* 1880. (Courtesy of the Kenton County Public Library.)

Viewed from the west, this image of the Cincinnati Southern Railway Bridge gives a rare view of the swing span on the southern end of the structure. It pivoted horizontally when opened, facilitating transit of river traffic when the water level made it otherwise impossible to pass under the bridge. The bridge was completed in 1877 by the Keystone Bridge Company. The swing span no longer exists on the current bridge (rebuilt in 1922), although the pier that once supported it still stands. (Courtesy of the Kenton County Public Library.)

## LUDLOW.

President Scott, of the Cincinnati Southern, has offered to build a footway on the bridge crossing the Ohio, if the expense, which is not to exceed $15,000, is borne by the citizens of Ludlow. The railroad company will charge toll at the rate of one cent for a single passage, or thirty tickets for twenty five cents.

The *Daily Commonwealth* newspaper on Friday, November 16, 1883, announced plans for a footway to be added onto the bridge connecting Ludlow and Cincinnati. However, a fee for the privilege would be charged—1¢ per passage! This brought to a close the multi-decade challenge Ludlow residents faced regarding transportation to Cincinnati. Ferry service had been expensive and unreliable; the road to Covington was perilous and at times impassable. Thus, the footway was great news for Ludlow, although it was not completed for use until 1885. (Courtesy of the Kenton County Public Library.)

Samuel Bodkin, engineer for the Cincinnati Southern Railway, is seen on the right in this impressive railroad image. The 1926 city directory shows him living at the Lagoon Park Apartments, the transformed clubhouse of the departed Lagoon Amusement Park. (Courtesy of the Louis Bodkin family.)

This well-preserved photograph displays members of the Cincinnati Southern Railway. Only the man on the far left is identified, J. McIntosh. (Courtesy of the Kenton County Public Library.)

Railroad shops in Ludlow are under construction in this photograph. The plant included car repair shops, car cleaning facilities, and a roundhouse. (Courtesy of the Kenton County Public Library.)

Labeled "fire of C.S.R.R. shops," this photograph was undated. Men are peering into a crater caused by a large explosion, and early firefighting equipment can be seen in the background. (Courtesy of the Kenton County Public Library.)

As seen in this 1914 photograph, two large water towers existed on the railroad grounds in Ludlow. Each tank had a capacity of 50,000 gallons; they were located near the intersection of Davies and Poplar Streets. (Courtesy of the Special Collections and Archives, Northern Kentucky University.)

This building was the oil house on railroad property, also photographed in 1914. The tops of the two water towers can be seen on the distant right. (Courtesy of the Special Collections and Archives, Northern Kentucky University.)

Ludlow resident Thomas W. Rohan and wife, Winifred (née Glenn), were photographed with their children in 1907. According to church records of St. James Church, they were married in 1893. Rohan was an engineer, and later foreman, for the Cincinnati Southern Railway. (Courtesy of the Rohan family.)

Pertinent in this photograph, taken from the hills behind the railroad property, is the roundhouse. The circular turntable in the center of the roundhouse rotated to allow transfer of locomotives into the building for storage or repair. (Courtesy of the Kenton County Public Library.)

Seen at Ash Street, the Southern Railway Bridge was rebuilt with a heavier steel structure in 1922. Creative planning allowed for the bridge to be kept in service during the reconstruction. (Courtesy of the Kenton County Public Library.)

The Ludlow Railroad Depot was photographed in 1973. Passenger service had been phased out after 1968, with arrivals and departures completely vanishing by 1972. The structure has since been demolished. (Courtesy of the Hellebush family.)

*Six*

# CHURCHES AND SCHOOLS

Early pupils of Ludlow Public School organize in front of the school building c. 1908. Prior to having a dedicated building of their own, classes were held for early Ludlow students on the first floor of the Ludlow Christian Church at Elm and Locust Streets. (Courtesy of the Earl Clark Collection.)

# TEACHER'S CERTIFICATE.

## THE EXAMINERS OF PUBLIC SCHOOLS

### ❧ IN LUDLOW, KY. ❧

*At a Regular Meeting of the Board, having Examined*

*Anita Davis*

IN SPELLING, ~~DEFINITIONS~~, READING, ENGLISH GRAMMAR, GEOGRAPHY, MENTAL ARITHMETIC, WRITTEN ARITHMETIC, PENMANSHIP, ~~AMERICAN HISTORY~~, THEORY AND PRACTICE OF TEACHING, ~~ALGEBRA~~, ~~NATURAL PHILOSOPHY, CONSTITUTION OF THE UNITED STATES, ANCIENT AND MODERN HISTORY~~, ~~ANATOMY, PHYSIOLOGY, LITERATURE, MUSIC, CIVIL GOVERNMENT, HISTORY OF KENTUCKY, NAR-~~ ~~COTICS, GEOLOGY, BOTANY, BOOKKEEPING, GEOMETRY, MENTAL PHILOSOPHY, LATIN, ETC.~~ *Eng. Composition and Drawing.*

*And having inspected* her *Credentials and Certificates of Character,* **do hereby Certify** *that* she *possesses the requisite qualifications to teach* A Primary *School, and that* she *has exhibited sufficient evidence that* she *sustains a good moral character, and has had _____ years' experience in teaching.*

**Given under our hands,** *this* 19th *day of* May 1897

| STUDIES. | Result. | STUDIES. | Result. |
|---|---|---|---|
| Spelling | 100 | Algebra | ----- |
| Reading | 98 | Geometry | ----- |
| Penmanship | 90 | Bookkeeping | ----- |
| English Grammar | 97 | Astronomy | ----- |
| Geography | 80 | Music | ----- |
| Mental Arithmetic | 60 | Chemistry | ----- |
| Written Arithmetic | 60 | Mental Philosophy | ----- |
| Drawing | 65 | Moral Philosophy | ----- |
| English Composition | 80 | Trigonometry | ----- |
| Physiology, Hygiene and Narcotics | 70 | Surveying | ----- |
| Theory and Practice of Teaching | 65 | Economics | ----- |
| Civil Government | 80 | Logic | ----- |
| Natural Philosophy | ----- | Geology | ----- |
| American History | ----- | Botany | ----- |
| English Literature | ----- | History of Kentucky | ----- |
| General History | ----- | | |
| Latin | ----- | Average, | 78⅞ |

*P H Duncan*
*Aaron Grady.*
*N. D. Jolly*

*Board of Examiners.*

*Valid for* one *years from date.*

Anita Davies was awarded a teacher's certificate in 1897 by the Examiners of Public Schools in Ludlow. (Courtesy of the Schachere family.)

This location of Ludlow Public School was built in 1895–1897 at Oak and Adela Streets on land donated by Albert and William Ludlow. Classes had moved from the Ludlow Christian Church location first to a school building on Linden Street, between Kenner and Davies Streets, in 1869. When the school outgrew the Linden Street facility, the pictured structure became home to Ludlow Public School. It was demolished in 1957; newer school buildings are currently located on the site. (Courtesy of the Kenton County Public Library.)

_Seventh_

_Annual Commencement_

_Ludlow High School_

_Thursday Evening,  June 17th., 1897_

_at_

_Odd Fellows Temple_

_Ludlow, Kentucky._

A program from the 1897 commencement ceremony for Ludlow High School lists the names of all five graduates. The school graduated its first class just eight years earlier, in 1889. Few know Ludlow High School by its official name—George Washington Memorial High School. (Courtesy of the Schachere family.)

_Graduates_

_Kate Adele Allensworth,_

_Charlotte Feed,_

_Kate Christina Goetz,_

_Anita Davies,_

_William Earl Grady,_

_We cordially invite you to be present_

Samuel Bodkin (left) is the only identified person in front of the wooden stands of Ludlow's early baseball park c. 1910. The park was located north of Victoria Avenue. (Courtesy of the Louis Bodkin family.)

A parade passes by as a new building is constructed on Ludlow school grounds at Oak and Adela Streets in 1915. (Courtesy of the Kenton County Public Library.)

| No. | NAMES OF PUPILS. 1897—1898 | Year of Entrance. | Age or Entering. | Course Taken. | Days Due. | Days Present. | Times Tardy. |
|---|---|---|---|---|---|---|---|

*F Grade, or 3rd year*
*Ludlow Public Schools*
*Mary A. Goetz, Teacher*

### F Grade. Boys.

| No. | Name | Year | Age | | 1st term | 2nd term | 1st term | 2nd term | Tardy |
|---|---|---|---|---|---|---|---|---|---|
| 1 | Ashworth, Richard | 1897 | ? | | 89 | 72 | 86 | 81½ | 0 |
| 2 | Anderson, Fred | " | 7 | | 91 | 77 | 91 | 94½ | 2 |
| 3 | Cason, Charles | " | 8 | | 91 | 97 | 91 | 96½ | 0 |
| 4 | Childs, Julius | " | 10 | | 91 | 72 | 86 | 82½ | 7 |
| 5 | Davis, Charles | " | 9 | | 91 | 77 | 70½ | 97 | 2 |
| 6 | Farley, Clyde | " | 11 | | 91 | 53 | 83½ | 42½ | 0 |
| 7 | Cull, Neil | " | 9 | | 91 | 77 | 91 | 77 | 3 |
| 8 | Hampton, Philip | " | 11 | | 82 | 77 | 79½ | 93 | 1 |
| 9 | Kling, Albert | " | 3 | | 77 | 77 | 90 | 77 | 0 |
| 10 | King, Andrew | " | 9 | | | | | | |
| 11 | Morris, Stanley | " | 3 | | 91 | 97 | 90½ | 77 | 0 |
| 12 | Mannum, George | " | 3 | | 91 | 77 | 91 | 77 | 8 |
| 13 | McGaugh, Thomas | " | 3 | | 85 | 77 | 81½ | 90 | 1 |
| 14 | Ritchie, Maurice | " | . | | 77 | 80 | 85 | 72 | 0 |
| 15 | Rockney, Charles | " | 9 | | 77 | 77 | 77 | 90 | 0 |
| 16 | Riggs, Eugene | " | 7 | | 91 | 97 | 91 | 77 | 1 |
| 17 | Short, Robert | " | 8 | | 91 | 77 | 88 | " | 0 |
| 18 | Triplett, Robert | " | 9 | | 91 | 77 | 90½ | 74 | 0 |
| 19 | Wells, Eugene | " | 10 | | 77 | 77 | 77 | 83 | 7 |
| 20 | Ward, Joel | " | 8 | | 91 | 77 | 87½ | 90½ | 0 |
| 21 | Weaver, William | " | 12 | | 89 | 97 | 79 | 94 | 2 |
| 22 | Wauger, George | " | 11 | | 56 | 77 | 54½ | 74½ | 2 |

A class roll from the 1897–1898 school year identifies Mary A. Goetz as the teacher of "F grade," or third year. In her honor, the elementary school is now known as Mary A. Goetz Elementary School. This page lists the names of the 22 boys in her class that year. (Courtesy of the Kenton County Public Library.)

## Girls. H Grade

| # | Name | Year | | Scores | | | | |
|---|------|------|---|---|---|---|---|---|
| 1 | Allensworth, Annie | 1897 | 8 | 91 | 97 | 77 | 73 | 6 |
| 2 | Burns, Tillie | " | 13 | 91 | 54 | 87½ | 48½ | " |
| 3 | Biel, Mabel | " | 8 | 91 | 75 | 87 | 92 | 10 |
| 4 | Cason, Nannie | " | 10 | 92 | 77 | | | |
| 5 | Chadderton, Ruth | " | 9 | 91 | 97 | 85 | 77 | |
| 6 | Childs, Maude | " | 8 | 7 | 81 | 77 | 43 | 7 |
| 7 | Deur, Ida | " | 9 | 83 | 77 | 13 | 47 | 1 |
| 8 | Euler, Ida | " | 8 | 91 | 77 | 84½ | 78 | 0 |
| 9 | Gilbert, Martha | " | 8 | 77 | 86 | 74½ | 86 | 0 |
| 10 | Goetz, Esther | " | 8 | 91 | 97 | 87½ | 96½ | 0 |
| 11 | Hoffman, Carrie | " | 8 | 91 | 77 | 87 | 77 | 4 |
| 12 | Sanders, Bessie | " | 8 | 91 | 97 | 87 | 77 | 7 |
| 13 | Lonergan, Fannie | " | 12 | 88 | 77 | 84 | 93 | 3 |
| 14 | Murphy, Mary | " | 9 | 91 | 97 | 91 | 97 | 0 |
| 15 | Ritchie, Ruth | " | 8 | 91 | 97 | 90 | 93½ | 0 |
| 16 | Rouse, Sada | " | 8 | 91 | 97 | 84 | 91 | 0 |
| 17 | Robinson, Elsie | " | 8 | 91 | 97 | 91 | 97 | 2 |
| 18 | Sabie, Jessie | " | 11 | 91 | 97 | 77 | 97 | 1 |
| 19 | Stanley, Gladys | " | 9 | 91 | 77 | 89 | 97 | 8 |
| 20 | Wells, Maude | " | 9 | 81 | 97 | 77 | 91 | 0 |
| 21 | Wehrman, Lena | " | 8 | 77 | 77 | 77 | 95½ | 1 |

A continuation of the class list for 1897–1898 records the names of the 21 girls of Miss Mary A. Goetz's early class. At this time, she was just four years into what would be a long teaching career in Ludlow. In 1919, the State Board of Education in Frankfort awarded her a "life certificate to teach school." (Courtesy of the Kenton County Public Library.)

Mary Goetz, seen here in later years, dedicated over 50 years of service to the people of Ludlow after joining the school system in 1894. She retired in 1947 after teaching three generations of students. She lived at 414 Elm Street and was a lifelong member of Wesley United Methodist Church. She died in 1964 and is buried in Spring Grove Cemetery. (Courtesy of Wesley United Methodist Church.)

Rev. Henry Looschelders is seen with the St. Boniface First Communion group in 1920. Reverend Looschelders was the church's pastor from 1905 until 1927. (Courtesy of Dave Schroeder.)

**Registrum Baptizatorum in Ecclesia** *Sancti Bonifacii, Mart.*

*in oppido Ludlow*      **Diœcesis** *Covingtoniensis*

| Nomen Familiæ. | A. D. Die Mensis. | REGISTRUM BAPTISMORUM. | Observanda. |
|---|---|---|---|
| Barnfather | 1872. 17. Nov. | *Ego infrascriptus baptizavi* **Bertham** *natam 26. Septembris 1872* ex *Jacobo Barnfather,* ex loco _____ et *Anna Girenbach,* ex loco _____ conjugibus *Patrini fuerunt Anna Schmit, nat. Hummel* = *Petrus Frieden, Pastor.* | |
| Rolsen. | A. Domini 1873 13. Febr. | *Ego infrascriptus baptizavi* **Bernhardum Josephum** *natum 11. Februarii 1873* ex *Francisco Ferdinando Rolsen* ex loco *Dammen, Magni Ducatûs Oldenburg* et *Anna Maria Gertrude Stuckenberg* ex loco *Althausen in Hannover / Germaniâ conjugibus* *Patrini fuerunt Joh. Bernh. Herzog et Maria Stuckenberg, nat. Roelker,* = *Petrus Frieden, Pastor.* | † *mortuus est Martii 29. 1874* |
| Behm. | 1873 27. Febr. | *Ego infrascriptus baptizavi* **Joannam Margaretham** *natam 25. Februarii 1873* ex *Adamo Behm* ex loco *Hoerdt in Bavaria (Germaniâ)* et *Sophia Hermann* ex loco *Dundorf in Wurtemberg / Germ. conjugibus* *Patrini fuerunt Franciscus Freye et Margaretha Braun* *Petrus Frieden, Pastor.* | |

Displayed is the first page of St. Boniface's baptism registries showing the parish's first three baptisms in 1872–1873. Performing the baptisms for the Barnfather, Rolsen, and Behm families at the newly founded St. Boniface Church was Rev. Joseph Frieden, the parish's first resident pastor. (Courtesy of Parish Archives.)

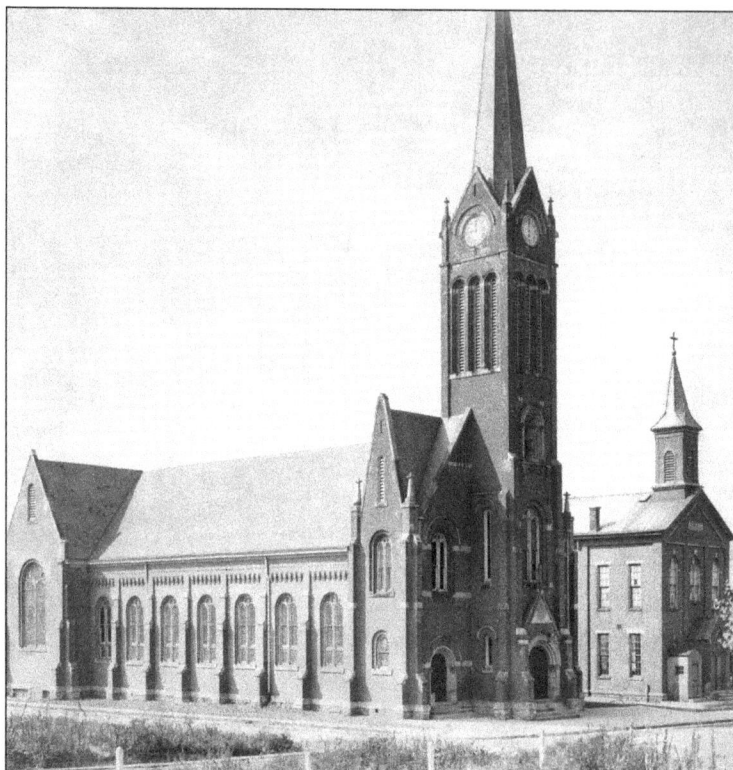

On the right stands the original St. Boniface Church, a rare view with the steeple still intact. Dedicated in 1872, this smaller building housed the school on the first floor and the church on the second floor. Classes were taught by the Sisters of Divine Providence. The larger church on the left was dedicated in 1893 and then rededicated in 1916, following rebuilding after major tornado damage in 1915. Both buildings still stand at Church and Adela Streets. (Courtesy of Parish Arhives.)

Pictured is a later view of the original St. Boniface building, less the steeple. The sign reads "St. Bonifacius Shule, errichted A.D. 1872." *Errichted* is the German word for erected or established. With *schule* being the German word for school, it's unclear why it is spelled *shule* on the building—an early spelling error, perhaps. St. Boniface School merged with St. James School in 1967 under Principal Sr. Rose Eileen (Mary) Maguire of the Sisters of Charity of Nazareth. (Courtesy of the Kenton County Public Library.)

The interior of St. Boniface Church was photographed around 1953. When established, this parish primarily served the German-speaking Catholics of Ludlow. St. Boniface is the patron saint of the Germans. He was murdered in Frisia (today part of the Netherlands) in 754 and is entombed at the cathedral in Fulda, Germany. (Courtesy of the Kenton County Public Library.)

A closer view inside St. Boniface Church shows the beautiful detail of the pulpit. (Courtesy of Parish Archives.)

On July 7, 1915, a tornado tore through the center of St. Boniface Church, leaving the steeple damaged yet surprisingly still erect. Reconstruction costs approached $30,000; much of this was obtained through various fund-raising efforts and donations from other Northern Kentucky parishes. (Courtesy of Parish Archives.)

Rev. Henry Looschelders stands among the ruins inside the church. During rebuilding, services were temporarily held in the school building. (Courtesy of the Kenton County Public Library.)

Another interior view of St. Boniface Church demonstrates the massive damage caused by the 1915 tornado. Incredibly it is reported that none of the statues in the church were damaged. (Courtesy of the Kenton County Public Library.)

St. James School originated on Oak Street in the building on the left, opening in 1893 with 125 pupils. The Sisters of Charity of Nazareth provided teachers. Previously the Odd Fellows' Hall, this building had many other prior occupants, including the Ludlow Presbyterian Church, the Wesley Methodist Congregation, and the Ludlow Mayor's Court. St. James Parish purchased the building in 1891 for $3,500. The structure was built around 1857 and was razed in 1911. St. James Church, seen on the right, was dedicated in October 1904. After St. Boniface merged with St. James in 1980, the church became home to the new combined parish. (From the collection of the Public Library of Cincinnati and Hamilton County.)

The above photograph shows the interior of St. James Church in 1904, at the time of dedication. As seen below, some embellishments had been added by the 1960s. Major interior renovation and modernization took place in 1981, including removal of the statues as well as the high and shrine altars. (Top courtesy of Dave Schroeder; bottom courtesy of the Kenton County Public Library; photographs by Raymond Hadorn, used with permission of the Hadorn family.)

On the steps of 323 Oak Street, the First Communion group of St. James Church is gathered with Rev. Clement Bocklage on June 8, 1930. Now a private residence, this house once served as the rectory and later was the convent for the Sisters of Charity of Nazareth. (Courtesy of the Schachere family.)

Established to serve the English-speaking Catholics of Ludlow, St. James Church was originally located in this building on the east side of Carneal Street, between Elm and Oak Streets. Previously the Armory Hall, this structure was purchased in 1887 and refurbished to accommodate church services. St. James parishioners met here until 1904. (Courtesy of Dave Schroeder.)

As seen on this program cover, St. James students performed in a play in April 1946. St. James had a high school from 1928 until 1948, with the last class graduating nine students. The elementary school existed much longer, surviving from 1893 until 1983. (Courtesy of the Kenton County Public Library.)

After establishment of St. James High School in 1928, the first class graduated in June 1932. Pictured from left to right are (first row) Eileen Reardon, Marian Hamilton, Ruth Kelly (first principal of the high school), Ida Belding, and Mary Margaret Lindsay; (second row) Catherine Mary Driscoll and Lucille Lenahan. From 1928 to 1942, classes were taught by lay teachers; Mother Ann Sebastian of the Sisters of Charity of Nazareth provided sisters for the school starting in 1942. Over the years, students came not only from St. James and St. Boniface Parishes in Ludlow, but also from other nearby parishes, including the Covington parishes of St. Aloysius, St. John, and St. Patrick, as well as St. Ann Parish in West Covington. The high school division of St. James School closed in 1948. (Courtesy of Dave Schroeder.)

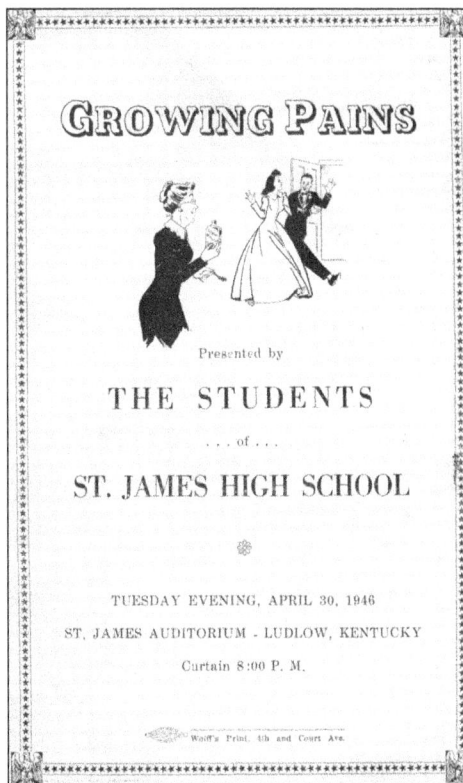

GROWING PAINS

Presented by

THE STUDENTS

... of ...

ST. JAMES HIGH SCHOOL

TUESDAY EVENING, APRIL 30, 1946
ST. JAMES AUDITORIUM - LUDLOW, KENTUCKY
Curtain 8:00 P. M.

Wolf's Print, 4th and Court Ave.

Wesley United Methodist Church (earlier Wesley Methodist Episcopal Church) was built in 1889. It was 1853, however, when the congregation originally organized, even before the city of Ludlow was chartered. Prayer groups met in private residences, including that of the Venn family. From 1857 to 1889, meetings and services were held in the Odd Fellows' Hall on Oak Street, which was located just across the street from the present-day church occupying 319 Oak Street. (From the collection of the Public Library of Cincinnati and Hamilton County.)

The Methodist men's group gathered c. 1921–1924. The church was under the direction of Pastor W. H. Davenport at this time. (Courtesy of Wesley United Methodist Church.)

Esther Goetz is shown with her Sunday school class in this undated photograph. Like her sisters, Mary and Christina Goetz, she was a teacher for the Ludlow public school system. Esther Goetz died in 1943 at the age of 53. (Courtesy of Wesley United Methodist Church.)

The steeples of St. James Church (left) and Wesley United Methodist Church (right) face each other in the 300 block of Oak Street. The churches were built 15 years apart, Wesley United Methodist in 1889 and St. James in 1904. A horse-drawn wagon is seen crossing Oak Street in the distance. (Courtesy of the Hellebush family.)

The original Ludlow Christian Church at Elm and Locust Streets was built in 1851 and demolished in 1895. Prior to this location, the congregation met in the Glaspohl family home starting around 1840, and then in a small building on Ash Street from 1846 to 1850. (Courtesy of the Kenton County Public Library.)

As a new Ludlow streetcar crosses in front of the old Ludlow Christian Church, a train passes behind it in 1894. The earliest classes of the Ludlow Public School were held on the first floor of this building until a separate school building was constructed on Linden Street in 1869. (Courtesy of the Kenton County Public Library.)

The demolishing of the old Ludlow Christian Church building was well underway on April 11, 1895. (Courtesy of the Kenton County Public Library.)

At the same location, the new Ludlow Christian Church was erected at the southeast corner of Elm and Locust Streets. The church was dedicated in January 1896. Although the building still stands, the church closed in 2005. (Courtesy of the Kenton County Public Library.)

The First Presbyterian Church of Ludlow at 429 Oak Street was dedicated on May 11, 1873. This site was built after an earlier church on Elm Street, utilized from 1870 to 1872, was destroyed by fire. The church was founded in 1867 with a congregation of six; membership was reported to be over 300 in the early 1950s. The congregation recently left Ludlow and is now known as the Community of Faith Presbyterian Church, located on Highland Pike in Covington. (Courtesy of the Kenton County Public Library.)

The baraca class of the First Presbyterian Church is seen c. 1916. Baraca classes were Bible classes for young men. (Courtesy of the Kenton County Public Library.)

Rev. J. J. Francis was pastor of the First Presbyterian Church *c.* 1905. (Courtesy of the Kenton County Public Library.)

After organizing in 1849, the original location of the First Baptist Church was on the east side of Carneal Street, north of Elm. Land for this structure was donated by William Hay. He was one of the city's original councilmen chosen during Ludlow's first election in 1864 and for whom Hay Street is named. This site was used until 1891. The structure has been modified but still stands today as a private residence at 19 Carneal Street. (Courtesy of the Kenton County Public Library.)

A very early photograph shows the Baptist Ladies' Sewing Society, photographed outside of the Ritchie residence at Elm and Locust Streets. (Courtesy of the Kenton County Public Library.)

Located on the northwest corner of Linden and Kenner Streets, Ludlow First Baptist Church was dedicated in 1891. It remains the current location of the church today, with several additions having taken place over the years. Both the church and its associated Sunday school are still very active in Ludlow today. (Courtesy of the Kenton County Public Library.)

The T.E.L. Class of Ludlow First Baptist Church was photographed in 1924. This was a Bible study class for women. T.E.L. stands for Timothy, Eunice, and Lois, from the Book of 2 Timothy 1:5. (Courtesy of First Baptist Church of Ludlow.)

Rev. Charles E. Nash was an early leader of the First Baptist Church, photographed here *c.* 1892. He led the church from 1890 until 1893. (Courtesy of the Kenton County Public Library.)

**STRAWBERRY FESTIVAL**

AND

**Mrs. Jarley's Wax Works,**

FOR THE BENEFIT OF THE

**FIRST BAPTIST CHURCH,**

LUDLOW, KY.

FRIDAY, JUNE 13th, 1873.

Admission, 25 Cents.

An 1873 ticket to an early fund-raiser for the Ludlow First Baptist Church shows admission to the Strawberry Festival to be 25¢. (Courtesy of First Baptist Church of Ludlow.)

The Glad Girls Class from Ludlow Baptist Church is shown in 1924. The church was under the direction of Rev. George B. Bush at the time. (Courtesy of First Baptist Church of Ludlow.)

The Fidelis Class of the First Baptist Church was a Bible study class for single women. Identified in this photograph is Dessie Hauck, standing third from the left. (Courtesy of First Baptist Church of Ludlow.)

# Seven

# LAGOON AMUSEMENT PARK

Riders take their seats on the miniature train ride at the Lagoon Amusement Park. The roller coaster is seen in the background, as well as its associated turnaround building on the far right. Listed in the city directory as a "pleasure resort," the park provided entertainment for individuals of all ages from 1895 to 1918. (Courtesy of the Hellebush family.)

This eye-catching structure served as the entrance to the Lagoon Amusement Park. Many postcards exist of this view with slight variations. The entrance site was located on what is now Laurel Street, just east of Lake Street. (Courtesy of the Terry W. Lehmann Collection.)

The large body of water known as the lagoon was made by damming Pleasant Run Creek, which ran to the Ohio River. Boaters, fishermen, and swimmers made use of the lake. (Courtesy of the Earl Clark Collection.)

This photograph features the boat landing and boathouse. Members of a canoe club also frequently met at the Lagoon Amusement Park. (Courtesy of the Hellebush family.)

The roller coaster paralleled the train trestle, as can be seen in this view of the park. A car filled with riders can be seen on the far left. (Courtesy of the Hellebush family.)

A season pass was issued to "Frank G. Sheppard & Lady" in 1895 for the park's opening season. It bears the signature of John J. Noonan, the first general manager of the amusement park. (Courtesy of the Terry W. Lehmann Collection.)

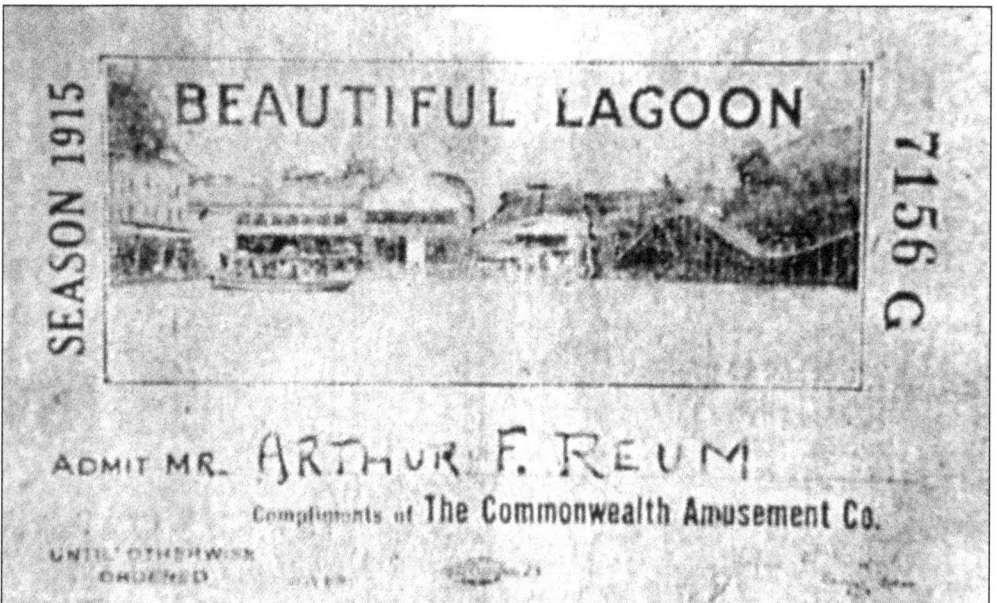

This park pass for the much-later 1915 season belonged to Arthur F. Reum. (Courtesy of the Earl Clark Collection.)

Both interior and exterior views of the electric merry-go-round are shown. This ride was reportedly constructed at a cost of $10,000. (Courtesy of the Hellebush family.)

The Automobile Aerial Road was advertised as "the only ride of the kind in the world"—where riders could experience "autoing in the tree-tops"! (Courtesy of the Hellebush family.)

AUTOING IN THE TREE-TOPS, AT BEAUTIFUL LAGOON,
LUDLOW, KY.
THE ONLY RIDE OF THE KIND IN THE WORLD.

A group identified as "Violet Weaver and friends" gets ready to experience the Automobile Aerial Road. Violet Weaver was the wife of Jerome J. Weaver, one of the original incorporators of the Lagoon Amusement Park. (Courtesy of the Hellebush family.)

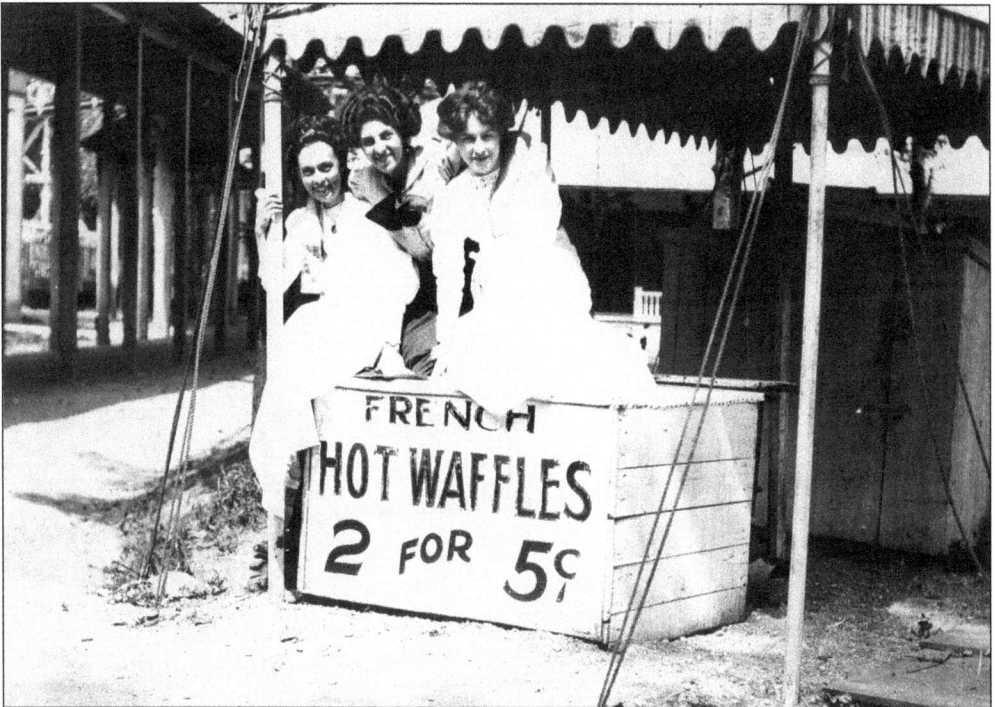

"Violet Weaver and friends" are seen again at the Hot Waffle stand. (Courtesy of the Hellebush family.)

The clubhouse at the Lagoon Amusement Park was widely photographed, with many old postcards still in existence. The postmark on this card was July 13, 1909. (Courtesy of Tom and Mary Kjelby.)

Kitchen workers pose outside of the clubhouse, which provided fine dining for park patrons. (Courtesy of Bill and Sharon Whiteley.)

An early view of Lake Street shows the clubhouse in the background. The family in the photograph is unidentified. In later years, the structure would be converted into apartment buildings. (Courtesy of Bill and Sharon Whiteley.)

The tiered veranda of the clubhouse faced the lake. (Courtesy of Bill and Sharon Whiteley.)

The Motordrome was constructed in 1913 to host professional motorcycle races, with advertisements proclaiming speeds up to 90 miles per hour. The quarter-mile track had a 60-degree incline. (Courtesy of the Hellebush family.)

A closer view of part of the Motordrome shows the spectator stands above the periphery of the saucer. Goodyear Tires took advantage of advertising space even in 1913. (Courtesy of the Hellebush family.)

An accident at the Motordrome in July 1913 led to much public controversy, as illustrated in this cartoon from the *Kentucky Post* on August 12, 1913. Odin Johnson of Salt Lake City lost control of his motorcycle and went over the guardrail, breaking through a wire barrier and soaring into the spectator stands. Reports claimed the vehicle hit a gas lamp, with a large explosion and fire ensuing. Despite these displays of public opinion, the Motordrome did reopen, however, with new requirements for slower speeds and improvements in the spectator barriers. (Courtesy of the Kenton County Public Library.)

Another drawing from the *Kentucky Post* on August 2, 1913, grimly expresses discontent with safety issues at the Motordrome. Nine deaths were directly caused by the fire, with several later attributed to injuries sustained that day. Many more were seriously injured in the estimated crowd of 5,000. Motordrome manager J. W. Eberhardt was charged with involuntary manslaughter but was later cleared of the charges. (Courtesy of the Kenton County Public Library.)

A man takes a rest among the amusements at the Lagoon Amusement Park in this postcard view, postmarked March 8, 1907. The impressive park would continue to host visitors for just over one more decade. (Courtesy of Tom and Mary Kjelby.)

A horse-drawn wagon of the Lagoon Amusement Park is stocked up with supplies in this undated photograph. (Courtesy of the Hellebush family.)

Construction is still underway in this view of the Shooting the Chutes ride. Participants traveled up the structure in cars, then slid down the waterslide in boats, landing in a pool of water. Built at a cost of $30,000, it was reported to be only the fifth one in the world, with others located in London, Milan, Antwerp, and Chicago. Frequent accidents made this a short-lived attraction. (Courtesy of the Hellebush family.)

Boats of all sizes enjoyed the lake at the Lagoon Amusement Park. Five small islands were scattered within the lake, and there was a sand beach for sunbathers. (Courtesy of the Hellebush family.)

# General Railway Employes' Reunion

## AT

# LAGOON,

## Saturday, September 16, 1899.

| | |
|---|---|
| | B. & O. S.-W.<br>C. L. Brevoort. |
| X | C. C. C. & St. L.<br>Thos. Doyle. |
| | C. H. & D.<br>J. L. Orbison. |
| | C. N. O. & T. P.<br>E. A. Sherman. |
| | C. & O.<br>J. N. Fry. |
| | L. & N.<br>Wm. Adair. |
| | P. C. C. & St. L.<br>S. Miller. |

Candidate receiving the largest number of votes will be awarded First Prize—A HANDSOME SILVER TEA SERVICE.
Candidate receiving the second largest number of votes will be awarded Second Prize—A ELEGANT SILVER WATER SERVICE.

Hennegan & Co.

COMPLIMENTARY.
ADMIT ONE.

An 1899 ticket to a railroad employees' gathering has survived over a century. (Courtesy of Jim Knipfer.)

At this booth, ring toss winners were awarded knives and pistols! Other attractions at the park included a penny arcade, a glass-blowing booth, and a Japanese tea garden. (Courtesy of the Hellebush family.)

Two photographs display the oversized Circle Swing. (Top courtesy of Carl Rekow; bottom courtesy of the Hellebush family.)

Ascension balloons were occasionally launched as part of the entertainment for park visitors. The railroad trestle that now crosses over Sleepy Hollow Road is seen in the background. (Courtesy of the Hellebush family.)

A rare view of the inside of the theater at the Lagoon Amusement Park also showcases advertisements of early Ludlow businesses. These include Amos Teed Shoes, J. S. McCormick (druggist), Monroe and Brashear Meat Market, Louis C. Lippert (druggist), John Miller Hardware, John Allison Livery, Buchanan Brothers (roofers), Julius Schmidt (plumber), M. Cleveland Groceries, A. R. Reichler Bakery and Confectionery, Gibbs and Robinson Groceries, William Nie (tailor), Arthur Teed Confectionery, C. H. Crigler (dentist), Barr and Mason Fire Insurance, John H. Boll (architect), and William R. Scheifers Dry Goods. (Courtesy of the Hellebush family.)

Amusement park patrons and workers pause for a quick photograph. Pictured from left to right are unidentified, George Pugh, "Pig Iron" Traylor, Orie Craner, and Alvie Gardiner. (Courtesy of the Hellebush family.)

Two pony tracks were located on amusement park grounds. Goat-drawn wagons are also seen in this photograph. (Courtesy of the Hellebush family.)

Naval battle reenactments with miniature replicas were just one of many special attractions occurring at the amusement park. The battery-powered models were often a part of firework shows. (Top courtesy of Ed Kleier; bottom courtesy of the Hellebush family.)

THE ROOF IS OFF
AT THE
LAGOON
BUT ALL AMUSEMENTS AND CONCESSIONS ARE OPEN FOR BUSINESS. 500 WORKMEN MAKING IT BETTER THAN EVER BEFORE. SEE THE CYCLONIC CHANGES TODAY.

Lagoon management tried to make light of a bad situation after a devastating tornado destroyed much of the park on July 7, 1915. This advertisement in the *Kentucky Post* on July 10, 1915, announces the park's reopening shortly after the disaster. (Courtesy of the Kenton County Public Library.)

The roof is indeed quite literally off in this photograph of the dance pavilion after the 1915 tornado. (Courtesy of the Hellebush family.)

More views of tornado damage make it hard to believe that the amusement park was ever able to reopen for business. Destruction and losses from the tornado were felt to have contributed to the park's eventual closure just several years later. (Courtesy of the Hellebush family.)

This view, taken from inside the center of the Motordrome, shows the collapse of a large portion of the racetrack as well as the upper spectator stands. (Courtesy of the Hellebush family.)

Two men appear shocked as they survey the widespread tornado damage at the Motordrome entrance in July 1915. (Courtesy of the Earl Clark Collection.)

The tornado showed no mercy for the Motordrome, the site of much controversy two years earlier. (Courtesy of the Hellebush family.)

For many years after the Lagoon Amusement Park had closed, the lake still remained a gathering place during winters as a popular ice-skating site. Houses along Lake Street are seen in the background. (Courtesy of the Hellebush family.)

This aerial view after all other remnants of the amusement park had disappeared shows the enormity of the lagoon. Ludlow is viewed on the left, with Bromley on the right. The lagoon was later gradually filled in, and the amusement park has become a distant yet mesmerizing memory. (Courtesy of the Hellebush family.)

Visit us at
arcadiapublishing.com

www.ingramcontent.com/pod-product-compliance
Lightning Source LLC
Chambersburg PA
CBHW050653150426
42813CB00055B/1979

9 781531 626358